Olivia Frey

Narrative Technique in Julian Barnes' "Art

Negotiating Truth and Fiction

GRIN - Verlag für akademische Texte

Der GRIN Verlag mit Sitz in München und Ravensburg hat sich seit der Gründung im Jahr 1998 auf die Veröffentlichung akademischer Texte spezialisiert.

Die Verlagswebseite www.grin.com ist für Studenten, Hochschullehrer und andere Akademiker die ideale Plattform, ihre Fachtexte, Studienarbeiten, Abschlussarbeiten oder Dissertationen einem breiten Publikum zu präsentieren.

Dokument Nr. V121837 aus dem GRIN Verlagsprogramm

Olivia Frey

Narrative Technique in Julian Barnes' "Arthur & George"

Negotiating Truth and Fiction

GRIN Verlag

Bibliografische Information Der Deutschen Bibliothek: Die Deutsche
Bibliothek verzeichnet diese Publikation in der Deutschen Nationalbibliografie;
detaillierte bibliografische Daten sind im Internet über http://dnb.ddb.de/
abrufbar.

1. Auflage 2009
Copyright © 2009 GRIN Verlag
http://www.grin.com/
Druck und Bindung: Books on Demand GmbH, Norderstedt Germany
ISBN 978-3-640-26574-9

322: Literary Seminar

"The 19th Century through Modern Eyes: Contemporary Neo-Victorian Novels"

WS 2008/09

Narrative Technique in

Julian Barnes' *Arthur & George*:

Negotiating Truth and Fiction

Olivia Frey

Table of Contents

1. Introduction

In his novel *Arthur & George* Julian Barnes not only recreates the lives of his two eponymous characters, but also minutely reconstructs the historical incident that made their lives intersect. In the long-forgotten and unsolved case of the Great Wyrley[1] Outrages in 1903, George Edalji (1877-1953), a half-Indian Birmingham solicitor, was wrongly convicted of animal mutilation and imprisoned. It was Sir Arthur Conan Doyle (1859-1930), the famous writer and inventor of Sherlock Holmes, who slipped into the role of a detective to investigate the truth behind the case and to help undo a miscarriage of justice.

On the one hand, the novel provides "the conventional pleasure of historical fiction" (Walter, par. 4) because it revolves around real-life figures and is based on a real incident. Applying his investigative skills, Barnes carefully researched their biographies and history, and represents them faithfully and meticulously. On the other hand, it has to be borne in mind that it is nevertheless a fictionalized representation shaped by Barnes' creative and imaginative skills. Thus, the "novel mixes reality and imagination so that the book is part history, part biography and part fiction" (Guignery 129). In terms of genre, *Arthur & George* could hence be classified as faction, "a work that is on the borderline between fact and fiction, concerned primarily with a real event or persons, but using imagined detail to increase readability and verisimilitude" (Hawthorn 64).

It is exactly this delicate relationship of proven facts and fictional creations Barnes plays with throughout the novel in order to expose "[t]he tenuous nature of reality and the fine line between truth and fiction" (Ball, par. 5). Therefore, *Arthur & George* could even be categorized as a postmodern novel which authentically represents history, while being aware of its own artificiality and questioning the dichotomy of fact and fiction as well as the claim to one objective truth. In this context, it is worth examining in how far this is reflected on the level of surface content as well as on the level of textualisation, particularly in terms of narrative technique, including discursive devices such as structure, narrative situation, modes of speech, thought and consciousness representation, intertextuality and metafiction.

2. The Structure: Where Truth Begins and Ends

Basically, the novel's surface structure is divided into four chapters, which are headed "Beginnings" (Julian Barnes[2] 1-64), "Beginning with an Ending" (65-287), "Ending with a Beginning" (289-451) and "Endings" (453-501). They literally take the reader from the

---

[1] Great Wyrley is a parish and village in the county of Staffordshire, England.
[2] In parenthetical references Julian Barnes' full name is given in order to distinguish it from "Jon Barnes."

beginnings of the two protagonists' biographies until the end of Arthur's life. Each of the four chapters contains several sub-sections, which are headed mainly "Arthur," "George, "George & Arthur" or "Arthur & George," and alternate primarily between the two protagonists' respective points of view. Furthermore, there are constant shifts between present tense and past tense, whereby the lines between endings and beginnings of different phases in life, and between past or historical truth and present or current representation are blurred. The reader might therefore get the impression that the topics addressed are of contemporary concern.

> We view the stories and their world as through a telescope, at once vividly present, yet infinitely distanced. […] But the problems that preoccupied George and Arthur […] – guilt and innocence, the operation of the criminal justice system, divided loyalties, prejudice, religious belief and the reality of death – engage us still and are unlikely to be solved […]. (James, par. 11)

2.1. Real and Imaginary Beginnings and Endings

Although the ampersand in the title might create the illusion that Arthur and George are together throughout the novel, the narrative is kept divided for more than half of the story. In the first chapter, "Beginnings," Arthur's and George's life stories are traced in parallel, but apart – they are completely unaware of each other. As if the pieces of two puzzles were put together one after the other, the steps in their personal developments, from their childhood to the beginning of Arthur's career as ophthalmologist and writer, and George's professional life as solicitor are presented methodically and chronologically in quickly alternating one- to three-page narrations, which are headed either "Arthur" or "George." However, this parallel unfolding of their lives is not a historical fact and works only in Barnes' fictional universe. The narration actually shifts back and forth between two periods because Arthur was born eighteen years before George in 1859 (see Guignery 127). This constant use of analepses and prolepses is highlighted by the use of the past tense for Arthur and the present tense for George, whose story therefore becomes more immediate and more vivid.

The alternating narrations also emphasize the differences of Arthur's and George's characters and ways of life right from the beginning: "[h]is novel begins as a pair of alternating biographies, a tale of opposites" (Adams, par. 3). In fact, they inhabit completely different worlds. George is realistic, rather unimaginative, expected to be truthful, and told to believe in Biblical stories, which his father considers as "the way, the truth and the life" (Julian Barnes 5), while George himself is convinced to find truth in the science of law (see 89-90). By contrast, Arthur appears to embody imagination, and trusts the truths conveyed in chivalric stories and medieval romances like the Arthurian legends, "designed to teach him the distinction between right and wrong" (5). These different notions of truth-telling and

2

story-telling already reflect the uncertain status of truth as well as its ambiguous relationship to fiction. It is not entirely clear where truth can actually be found, but the solutions offered here imply that, for some people, it is conveyed by fictional stories in which they believe.

The second chapter, "Beginning with an Ending," continues the alternations between Arthur and George[3], and offers a full account of the prosecution against George from 1903 to 1906, as well as insights into the developments in Arthur's private and professional life between 1887 and 1906. As to George, the "Beginning" presumably refers to the first animal mutilations in 1903, which then lead to his arrest, trial and incarceration, while the "Ending" alludes to his release in 1906. The sections about George are told in the present tense until "the last normal twenty-four hours of his life" (129), but from his arrest onwards, his narrative switches to the past tense until his release. This change of tense probably indicates that "the progress of his life, as he sees it, comes to an unscheduled stop [...]" (Rafferty 3).

As regards Arthur, beginning and ending are very likely to refer mainly to his extramarital, yet platonic relationship with Jean Leckie starting in 1897 and to the death of his first wife Touie in 1906 respectively. However, this new stage in Arthur's life only sets in in the last sub-section of this chapter (see Julian Barnes 225-287), which goes back to 1897. From this point onwards, Arthur's narrative always changes to the present tense when Jean turns up, most likely to indicate that his love for her marks the beginning of a new chapter in his life, and "has no past, and no future [...]; it has only the present" (237).

Due to this analepsis from 1906 back to 1897, "the chronology of events is [...] disrupted" (Guignery 128), which is confirmed, for example, by the fact that in one of the sections about George, *The Hound of the Baskervilles* is alluded to by "the footprints of a gigantic hound" (Julian Barnes 119), and George in prison in 1904 reads "a tattered cheap edition" (164) of this novel. Thus, traces of Arthur can already be found in George's life, and they actually constitute first glimpses of their intersecting lives. However, it is only ninety-two pages later, in the part about Arthur, that the narrator mentions the composition of this book in 1901: "he resuscitates Sherlock Holmes and despatches him in the footprints of an enormous hound" (255-256). Nevertheless, at the end of this chapter the two parallel narrations coincide temporally for the first time, when Arthur receives a letter from George in 1906, in which he asks him for help (see 287).

Among these alternations mainly between George and Arthur, this chapter includes a section called "George & Arthur" (100-102), which establishes a link between the two

---

[3] Except for the sections on Inspector Campbell, the man at the head of the police investigation (see Julian Barnes 104-113, 119-126, 130-138).

protagonists for the first time without directly referring to them, and therefore without their being aware of it. Using a camera-eye technique, this sub-chapter consists of a rather neutral description of a man who crosses a field at night and goes towards a horse, to which he does something, and then disappears. "The reader is meant to think that this person doesn't sound like either George or Arthur, so it's probably someone else. Yet on the other hand, it says, "George & Arthur" there on the page. This must mean the incident has something to do with both of them, and is a tip-off that they will eventually meet" (Schiff 67). It also gives the reader a first hint to *what* will ultimately link their lives inextricably – the animal mutilations. Thus, in fictional or even metaphorical terms, the intersection of their lives starts at this point in 1903, while in historical terms, their paths cross only in 1906, that is at the end of the second and the beginning of the third chapter.

The third chapter, "Ending with a Beginning," basically traces Arthur's involvement in George's case from 1906 to 1907. The heading implies circularity: an ending obviously means a new beginning, the beginning of a new story or episode in life. In this particular context, the "Ending" obviously refers again to George's release from prison, while the "Beginning" marks the beginning of their intersecting lives and of George's life as a free man. It is probably also an allusion to Arthur's intention to "go back to the very beginnings of the case" (316) in order to find out the truth about the Great Wyrley Outrages and to prove George's innocence.

Headed "Arthur & George" (291-306), the first sub-section mirrors the novel's title and makes Arthur's and George's lives intersect directly for the first time, when Arthur agrees to take up the case. The two strands of narrative are finally brought together. At this point, the novel has obviously reached some sort of climax, which is emphasized by the use of the present tense. This chapter mainly[4] features narrations in which the foci of Arthur and George alternate within one sub-section, supposedly to draw attention to their relatedness. Moreover, these sections are characterized by a slow and unstable shift from the past to the present, which probably marks the difficult beginning of George's life in freedom. "George & Arthur" (415-427) relates their second meeting, in which George subtly criticizes Arthur's way of investigation[5], still using the past tense. This encounter is actually invented by Barnes to show that their relationship was not always positive and "to make this actual crossing point between their lives slightly longer and richer than it was" (Schiff 66). The narration then moves to the present tense like in "Arthur & George" (427-441), in which George is granted the important,

---

[4] Apart from three sections alternating between Arthur (see Julian Barnes 306-366, 392-415) and Captain Anson, the Chief Constable of Staffordshire (366-392).
[5] See chapter 4.2.3. (p. 18).

yet ambivalent free pardon[6], whereas "George & Arthur" (441-451) begins in the past tense, but suddenly switches to the present tense for their third meeting at Arthur's and Jean's wedding in 1907. This not only marks a new phase in Arthur's life, but also in George's: the invitation to the wedding symbolizes George's readmission to society (see 444).

The last part, "Endings," consists of a single section focusing on George's point of view and shifts 23 years forward to 1930, to the end of Arthur's life. At first told in the past tense, the narration suddenly changes to the present tense for Arthur's spiritualist memorial service – presumably to highlight the appearance of Arthur's and other people's spirits, which imply ever-present eternity. Furthermore, the present tense also puts emphasis on George's presence, which Barnes made up to maintain at least a symbolic link between the two protagonists until the end of the story (see Schiff 67-68), as well as on the fact that his life does not end in fictional terms. It is only in the author's note that his death in 1953 in mentioned (see 504). Arthur's death, on the other hand, does not really mark the end of his existence in a spiritualist sense. In the author's note, Julian Barnes declares that "Arthur continued to appear at seances around the world for the next few years" (503). So it is not really clear when Arthur's life is over – his life has obviously more than one end – and that is probably the reason why the plural "Endings" is used in the chapter heading.

In summary, already the structure deals with the relationship of fact and fiction, which is also mirrored in Arthur and George themselves, especially in their different conceptions of truth. Moreover, there are invented situations throughout the novel, in which Barnes "fiddled the record […] to make it work better in fictional terms" (Schiff 74) and to give his narrative more coherence. Many situations in which he obviously took imaginative freedom deal with the meetings between Arthur and George, and therefore raise questions about when and where their lives really intersect for the first and last time, or, to put it differently, where the metaphorical, fictional or historical truth about the story of Arthur and George begins or ends.

2.2. The Metafictional and Metaphorical Dimension

Working on a metafictional level, the novel's structure raises issues about literary structure, for example, questions about where a story begins and ends, whether a beginning does always have an ending, or whether an ending does not also imply the beginning of a new story. Most importantly, the structure "echoes the method of composition of Conan Doyle, who always conceives the conclusion of his stories first" (Guignery 128). He always knows where he is going when beginning a novel: "'Dr Doyle invariably conceives the end of his story first, and

---

[6] See chapter 4.2.4.

writes up to it.' [...] [I]t is as plain as a packstaff. How can you make sense of the beginning unless you know the ending? It's entirely logical when you reflect upon it" (Julian Barnes 75).

Arthur's approach to writing fiction is reflected on several layers of the story level. Firstly, the police's and Arthur's technique of investigation[7] mirror the composition of Arthur's novels. Both establish an outcome, a preconceived truth, and then make the facts and evidence fit this conclusion. Secondly, as the future creator of fictional realities, Arthur tends to view "his life in terms of stories and narratives" (Guignery 128). He is constantly struggling with the problem of how to conduct his life in order to get from its beginning to its predetermined end: "Arthur could see the beginning of the story – where he was now – and its happy end; only the middle was for the moment lacking" (Julian Barnes 7). Moreover, in the context of Arthur's interest in spiritualism, this metafictional comment even assumes a metaphysical quality because Arthur uses it to talk about the meaning of life as such: "And what is the point of life unless you know what happens afterwards? How can you make sense of the beginning if you don't know what the ending is?" (269).

In this context, it is worth having a close look at the novel's beginning and ending because it is there that the metaphorical level comes in. The opening sentence, "A child wants to see. It always begins like this, and it began like this then. A child wanted to see" (3), introduces a metaphor of sight and vision[8], of the ability to see the truth. It is echoed throughout the novel until the end, which consists of three unanswered questions: "What does he see? What did he see? What will he see?" (501). Thus, the ending does not really provide a neat closure and a solution to the mysteries of life or the Great Wyrley Outrages. On the contrary, the three open questions repeat and intensify the allusions to sight and vision, and the novel actually ends where it started. "The ending echoes the novel's beginning [...] and makes sense of it [...] by inflecting it with doubt, suggesting that the proper end of a true mystery story can only be a deepened sense of the mystery of what we have seen or are seeing or will see" (Rafferty 3). Therefore, beginning and ending only seemingly form a pair of opposites. In fact, they close the circle, which again makes it difficult to draw the line between them. Ironically, this open end also mocks Arthur's way of writing novels, investigation and life, in which the conclusion or ending is always predetermined: "Doyle, you cannot make sense of the ending until you know the beginning" (Julian Barnes 383), as Captain Anson put it.

---

[7] See chapters 4.2.1 and 4.2.3. respectively.
[8] See chapter 3.2.

On another level, the issue of beginning and ending can be applied to the quest for truth, to the question where one truth ends and another one begins. This is not only mirrored on the discourse level, in particular as regards the novel's structure, but also constantly echoed on the story level – be it the truth about the mystery of the Great Wyrley Outrages, life and death, spiritualism or love. This problem comes especially to the fore in the context of narrative situation and of speech, thought and consciousness representation, as is examined in the next chapter.

3. Narrator and Characters: Does Anybody See the Truth?

3.1. Narratorial Omniscience and Limitation

As regards the narrative situation, *Arthur & George* features a heterodiegetic third-person omniscient narrator, who is not present as a character and tells the story mainly as seen through the eyes of the two protagonists. Right from the beginning, he moves from Arthur's to George's limited point of view and vice-versa, either between or within the respective sub-sections. In this way their two subjective perspectives and distinct voices are juxtaposed right from the beginning. "The novel swings, in pendulum-like fashion, between the points of view of Arthur [...] and George [...], who could not be more different in personality, motivation, appearance, and capabilities. Their beliefs and perspectives on the world frequently clash [...]" (Holmes 58-59).

In addition, the points of view of secondary characters are occasionally introduced. Partly they are presented in separate sub-sections, such as Inspector Campbell (see Julian Barnes 104-113, 119-126, 130-138), or Captain Anson (see 366-392); partly their voices come up within the sections devoted to Arthur, George, Campbell or Anson – for example, George's father Shapurji Edalji, Arthur's mother, his second wife Jean Leckie or his secretary Alfred Wood. Hence the narrator is able to play in this fictional universe by slipping easily in and out of the characters' minds, thereby nearly blurring the distinction between narrator and character, between objective, faithful representation and subjective, fictionalized point of view. All these multiple voices result in polyphony, that is a variety of different subjective opinions, all of which claim truth for themselves, but actually relativize or even undermine each other. "[T]he story unspools in a variety of voices and points of view, all jostling for narrative pre-eminence, bickering among themselves about the truth" (Jon Barnes 1), as is discussed especially in chapters 3.2. and 4.2.

However, it is important to note that the narrator's omniscience is actually a psychological one and consists in "having complete access to his protagonists' inner lives, but [...] maintain[ing] a Flaubertian detachment" (Holmes 59). This basically means that his narrative voice is covert and largely restrained. He neither refers to himself nor addresses the reader directly, keeps himself back, lets the characters act and speak, and does not really manipulate them.

In this context, an important discursive device is free indirect discourse[9], "which combine[s] features of the characters' direct speech with those of the narrator's indirect reports" (Holmes 59). Using this way of psychological introspection, the narrator aims to empathically inhabit the characters' world of thoughts and feelings, thereby giving the reader a vivid insight into their minds and creating rich and believable inner lives. In many of these instances of free indirect discourse, the characters question the existence of absolute truth as well as the difference between knowledge and faith, or between reality and fiction. For example, George is impressed by Arthur's full conviction of his innocence, but at the same time questions the status of his own knowledge.

> His champion's words: I do not think, I do not believe, I *know*. Sir Arthur carried with him an enviable, comforting sense of certainty. He knew things. What does he, George, know? Does he finally know anything? What is the sum of knowledge he has acquired in his fifty-four years? [...] [H]e thinks a lot of things, he believes a few, but what can he really claim to know? (Julian Barnes 499)

3.2. Dialogues: Negotiating the Truth

As described in chapter 2.2., a metaphor of sight and vision, of the attempt to see clearly and to distinguish facts and truth from fiction and lies, plays a crucial role in *Arthur & George* right from the beginning until its open end, and refers to the unresolved questions about different topics dealt with in the novel:

> Arthur & George is a novel about sight in all of its forms. From the simple impact of optical myopia[10] to the complex impact of metaphorical myopia – short sightedness and long sightedness. It is about what we do and don't see: the visible bonds of friendship, sympathy, or hatred and prejudice. This sight extends to questions of guilt

---

[9] In this mode of thought and consciousness representation, which is also called narrated monologue, the narrator talks of the character in the third person and reports his or her words or thoughts by using his or her mind style. Although the scene is set by the narrator, the character's thoughts are conveyed more directly, immediately, and in a manner the character is likely to think. The syntax can become more informal, for example by the use of ellipses or exclamations. Actually we hear a dual voice because the narrator's and the character's voices merge (see Lethbridge and Mildorf 71-72; Jahn N 8.6).

[10] George's astygmatic myopia is considered to be the decisive piece of evidence to prove his innocence: because of his defective eyesight, he could not have gone to the field during the night and mutilated the horse. Dr Scott, who examined George's eyes, declared: "Like all myopics, Mr Edalji must find it at all times difficult to see clearly any objects more than a few inches off, and in dusk it would be practically impossible for him to find his ways about any place with which he was not perfectly familiar" (Julian Barnes 337).

and innocence; how we judge and determine, and perhaps more broadly, how each of us lives our lives with the knowledge of our impending death. (Ball, par. 1)

As a consequence, this metaphor establishes a connection between the three layers of the story level, which are dealt with in chapters 3.2.1., 3.2.2. and 3.2.3. respectively. They all revolve around the difference between believing and knowing and the often unsuccessful search for truth. In order to illustrate this, the many passages written in the form of dialogue serve as illuminating examples because the quest for absolute knowledge as well as the metaphor of sight and vision are embedded in them. They most likely have the function of presenting different views in a balanced way and of negotiating truth. The individual characters believe to be able to see the absolute truth, which is, however, only their subjective conviction. However, the narrator does generally not intrude in order to provide the readers with a definite answer to the questions about guilt or innocence, spiritualism or love. In fact, they are left with mysteries to solve on their own.

> Barnes's undramatized third-person narrator does not correct their misperceptions and prejudices in order to provide readers with a broader understanding of reality. [...] [T]he narrator refuses to pronounce authoritatively on matters that are in dispute, to offer moral judgements, or to clear up all of the novel's mysteries and uncertainties. (Holmes 59)

3.2.1. Guilt vs. Innocence: One Man's Truth Is Another Man's Lie

The foreground story is about the unsuccessful attempt to solve the mystery of the Great Wyrley Outrages and to insure justice: "it's [...] about the difference between what you think and what you can prove. You think someone's guilty, you believe they're guilty, but how can you *know* they're guilty, how can you prove they're guilty?" (Schiff 70).

In their debate about the Edalji case, Arthur's and Captain Anson's convictions of George's innocence and guilt respectively are contrasted, but neither of them is able to present his arguments as the strongest or even true ones because they continually counter each other. For instance, Anson ridicules Arthur's investigation of the case by comparing it to a Sherlock Holmes crime story, and considers his analysis as a highly speculative, unrealistic and even fictional "series of mistakes" (Julian Barnes 372). Moreover, he accuses him of having based his conviction of George's innocence, just like his writing, upon intuitive feelings, while he himself based his conclusion on "the consequences of police observations and reports over a number of years" (374). Arthur counters by reproaching him for having "made the boy a target from the beginning" (374) without any solid evidence, and uses George's professional and intellectual abilities as a solicitor, who has written several articles and a book, as a further

proof of his innocence (see 375). In turn, Anson tries to undermine Arthur's – and probably also the readers' – belief in George's honesty and innocence by showing a letter which attests to his concealed debts (see 378). Arthur, however, regards its content merely as a "desperate appeal of an honourable young man let down by his generosity" (379). The conversation continues in a similarly dialectical manner about issues such as George's half-Parsee background and social, family or sexual life, all of which are, according to the police, decisive factors. Yet, it is Anson who at some point sums up the main message of this dialogue, namely the fact that absolute truth and proof, such as in Arthur's detective fiction, are impossible in the real world: "I am not making some philosophical argument, I am being practical. What we know, what we end up knowing, is – enough to secure a conviction. Forgive me for lecturing you about the real world" (382).

3.2.2. The Uncertainty of Love

As regards the second story level, Arthur Conan Doyle's emotional life, especially the ten years during which he had a relationship with Jean Leckie, while his wife Touie was suffering from tuberculosis, "we ask ourselves exactly the same questions [...]: We think we're in love, we believe she loves us, but how can we *know*? How can we prove it? Can we ever prove it, and what is proof, what is knowledge?" (Schiff 70).

For instance, Arthur discusses the nature of love with his mother, whether it is a phenomenon of eternal duration or just a fluctuating emotion, and whether it can be objectively proved or just felt individually. In this dialogue, Arthur confesses that he is absolutely uncertain about his own personality, feelings and abilities: "I doubt everything. I doubt I ever loved Touie. I doubt I love my children. I doubt my literary capability. I doubt Jean loves me" (Julian Barnes 263). His mother, however, is convinced that Jean loves him, but Arthur again questions the existence and provability of absolute truth: "I think she does. I believe she does. How can I know she does? [...] I think it, I believe it, but how can I ever know it? If only I could prove it, if either of us could prove it" (264). All of his mother's attempts at convincing him of his love for Jean and vice versa, fail, and she ultimately concedes that belief, trust and personal conviction are more important than absolute knowledge or proof, which might not even exist: "[p]erhaps the best we can manage is thinking and believing. Perhaps we only truly know in the hereafter" (264). In order to emphasize that the truth about love cannot be uncovered, the discussion ends openly because "[s]ensibly, the Mam does not reply" (265) to Arthur's final expression of doubt.

3.2.3. In Search of Spiritual Truth

The third story level revolves around Arthur's interest in spiritualism or, as he prefers to call it, "spiritism" (Julian Barnes 265). In his view, it allows humans to see "the invisible and the impalpable, which lie just below the surface of the real [...] "(277), and to know and prove that the spirit survives the physical death. "If spiritualism were submitted to rigorous scientific examination and passed that test, this would [...] go beyond thinking and believing into knowing and proving" (Schiff 70). However, the readers are not expected to "accept Arthur's point of view [...] as authoritative. Sceptics [...] critique and counterbalance Arthur's views" (Holmes 64).

For example, in a discussion with his sister Connie, their opposing views are outlined, negotiated, but neither reconciled nor obliterated by one another. Connie, on the one hand, believes in the teachings of the church, considers it as the one and only alternative and distrusts the reliability of spiritism, which for her is a deceptive discipline (see Julian Barnes 269-270). She believes spiritist experiences to be "a wonderful story, and [her brother] a wonderful storyteller" (273), thereby turning his truth into a fiction. Arthur, on the other hand, tries to convince her of the value of spiritism, by countering that only a lot of it is treacherous, and that it is not about belief and faith, but rather about finding "the clear white light of knowledge" (270) by applying scientific methods: "[t]he whole point of psychical research [...] is to eliminate and expose fraud and deceit. [...] If you eliminate the impossible, what is left, however improbable, must be the truth "(270).

A similar 'dialogue' takes place within Arthur's second wife, Jean Leckie, herself. At first, she is upset that Arthur, whom she regarded as the incarnation of reason, feels attracted by this discipline of trances and crystal balls pretending to allow people to look into the soul, the future or higher spheres. Barnes textualizes her frustration by means of psychonarration[11]: "Inwardly, she has shuddered at the vulgarity and stupidity of that world [...]. And it has nothing to do with religion, which means morality. And the notion that this ... mumbo-jumbo appeals to her beloved Arthur is both upsetting and barely credible" (361). However, towards the end of the novel, she has developed a positive attitude towards spiritism. This becomes particularly apparent at the public spiritualist farewell on the occasion of Arthur's death. There she expresses her conviction that Arthur's spirit still exists and can be seen and

---

[11] In this mode of thought and consciousness representation, also known as narrative report of thought or narrated perception, the heterodiegetic narrator summarizes the character's conscious or unconscious perceptions, thoughts and feelings, and refers to him or her with third-person pronouns. The narrator usually uses his own voice, complete and ordered sentences and vocabulary. He may also add some remarks, which often creates distance between the reader and the character because the level of mediation remains obvious (see Lethbridge and Mildorf 71; Jahn N 8.11).

communicated with by means of clairvoyance, that is the eyes of faith and of the soul, which echo the metaphor of sight and vision: "Although our earthly eyes cannot see beyond the earth's vibrations, those with the God-given extra sight called clairvoyance will be able to see the dear form in our midst" (481). Consequently, Jean seems to have found her own truth about spiritism, but this is again not an absolute one – it is by no means valid for all the other characters.

In order to show that spiritism is presented as a contested discipline throughout the novel, Barnes lets it end on a discordant note. George's inconclusive thoughts about the appearance of spirits at Arthur's memorial service are discursivized via psychonarration, which again implies subjectivity. However, he is actually unable to establish his own truth about spiritism because he is full of ambivalent impressions: "He does not know whether he has seen truth or lies, or a mixture of both. He does not know if the clear, surprising, un-English fervour of those around him this evening is proof of charlatanry or belief. And if belief, whether true or false" (500).

4. Intertextuality: Multiple Truths Under Construction

"Apart from Jean's letter to Arthur, all letters quoted, whether signed or anonymous, are authentic; as are quotations from newspapers, government reports, proceedings in Parliament, and the writings of Sir Arthur Conan Doyle," Julian Barnes declares in the author's note (505). This statement immediately gives the reader a rough idea of the enormous amount of detailed research Barnes conducted on Sir Arthur Conan Doyle's and George Edalji's biographies as well as on the Great Wyrley Outrages before writing *Arthur & George*. Apart from serving as a starting point for the novel, all these public and private materials are also incorporated in it by means of numerous intertextual references. Nevertheless, the fact that Barnes considers it necessary to confirm the authenticity of his documents shows that they only form the red thread in his *fictional* account of the chronology of events.

4.1. Arthur & George: Real or Fictional Characters … or Both?
The fact that Arthur and George are real-life characters performing as the protagonists of a novel "gives him lots of opportunity for ruminations on the tricky boundaries between fiction and reality […]" (Walter, par. 6). Given that both characters are historical, it would, on the one hand, stand to reason that probably too much about them is known in order for creative imagination to unfold itself. On the other hand, it might exactly be the novelist's literary

creativity which makes it quite difficult for the reader to distinguish facts from fiction. However, it seems that it is exactly Barnes' intention to erase the line between historical evidence and imaginative fabrication of his characters.

In general, Barnes tries to authenticate Arthur's life, by quoting, for example, from his autobiography *Memories and Adventures*, published in 1924 (see Julian Barnes 470-472), which also contains an account of his involvement in the Edalji case, as well as from his literary works, such as *Sherlock Holmes*[12] in general, and *The Doings of Raffles Haw* (see 60), *Micah Clarke* (see 75) or *The Hound of the Baskervilles*[13] (see 119, 164, 256) in particular. Additionally, the novel includes a reproduction of the invitation for George to Arthur's and Jean's wedding (see 444) as well as extracts from articles about Arthur's death in 1930 in the *Daily Herald* (see 455-457).

Apart from tracing Arthur's life, Barnes also tries to empathize with him and represent his thoughts and feelings convincingly. As described in chapters 3.1. and 3.2., Barnes uses free indirect discourse and psychonarration as a means to fictionalize the characters' inner worlds. For example, Arthur's emotions about the lies he has told about his secret relationship with Jean make him feel "a hypocrite; [...] a fraud. In some ways, he has always felt a fraud, and the more famous he has become, the more fraudulent he has felt. He is lauded as a great man of the age, but though he takes an active part in the world, his heart feels out of kilter with it" (284). By contrast, Jean herself trusts him and characterizes him as "a man of honour" (310). Being given such opposing views of one character via fictionalized auto- and altero-characterization, the reader might find it difficult to determine for himself what Arthur was really like, what the truth about his personality is.

As regards George, Barnes includes, for instance, a replica of the title page of his book *Railway Law for the "Man in the Train"* (93), a manual on the rights of the travelling public published in 1901, as well as an extract of his article about the case, which appeared in the *Daily Express* in 1934 (504-505). Apart from other newspaper articles he wrote and Doyle's accounts of him, these are the only historical records of George (see Hanks, par. 4): as he is not as well documented as Arthur, he is definitely the greater fictional creation. In particular, "the prison section reminds us that there is far more to *Arthur & George* than a stringing together of facts" (Crumey, par. 11). It is a period in his life during which he feels that his world of logic and truth falls apart, and experiences a phase of conflicting emotions. In this

---

[12] See chapter 4.2.3.
[13] See chapter 2.1. (p. 3).

context, Barnes tries to communicate his own picture of George's inner world by offering an imagined, yet seemingly authentic insight into his mind, again by means of psychonarration:

> Part of him wanted to stay in his cell, plaiting nose-bags and reading the works of Sir Walter Scott, catching colds when his hair was cut in the freezing courtyard, and hearing the old joke about bed-bugs again. He wanted this because he knew it was likely to be his fate, and the best way to be resigned to your fate was to want it. The other part of him, which wanted to be free tomorrow, which wanted to embrace his mother and sister, which wanted public acknowledgement of the great injustice done him – this was the part he could not give full rein to, since it could end by causing him the most pain. (Julian Barnes 213)

In conclusion, the insertion of intertextual references to the two protagonists' lives implies authenticity in terms of biographical facts, and is "a reminder [...] that the novel is closely based on fact" (Crumey, par. 6). The fictionalized inner lives have a reality effect in terms of character psychology. By using "his licence as a novelist to try and imagine what the two protagonists were thinking or feeling, or to invent conversations [...]" (Guignery 130), Barnes constructs moving characters in whose emotional and mental states everybody is likely to believe. Therefore, the dichotomy of fact and fiction also exists on the level of characters, which is, however, only one of the numerous aspects "creating a space where [Barnes'] imagination can thrive" (Hanks, par. 1).

4.2. The Edalji Case: A Contested and Unfinished Story

In order to arrive at a faithful reconstruction of the Edalji case, Julian Barnes quotes from or mentions various authentic documents that played a significant role in it. In general, the continual use of intertextuality renders Barnes' literary representation of the case highly authentic and realistic in terms of historical evidence. Somehow Barnes himself slips into the role of a historical detective who minutely reconstructs the past like a crime. However, the regular insertion of quotes, allusions and references to letters, witness accounts, newspaper clippings and extracts from official documents also creates ambiguity. Embedding historical reality in a work of fiction, Barnes questions the status of historical truth, and "the seamless way in which these facts are woven into a compelling narrative" (Crumey, par. 6) makes it rather difficult for the reader to distinguish facts from fiction.

Apart from that, the various intertextual elements also entail polyphony, and by implication, the impossibility of establishing one absolute truth. Many subjective opinions or even truths are voiced, and often contradict and therefore destabilize each other. In this way, the reader is given a quite varied and balanced picture – not only about the question of guilt or innocence, but also about George himself and his personality. It is exactly this diversity of

diverging opinions and representations which makes it probably quite challenging to decide which one(s) to believe or adopt, or even leads to doubt whether absolute truth can be discovered at all. In order to illustrate the construction and malleability of truth as well as the novel's contrapuntal nature, the different voices and opinions, which are usually presented as subjective truths, are presented and examined in the following sub-chapters.

4.2.1. The Police Make Up a True Story

The Edalji case actually starts in 1892-1896, a period during which George's half-Parsee family, among other people in Great Wyrley, receive a series of anonymous menacing and obscene religious and racist hate mail (see Julian Barnes 47, 48, 56, 63), and become the target of newspaper hoax advertisements[14]. The local police immediately suspects George, probably because of racial prejudice or his isolated and seemingly odd way of life. In 1903, the hate campaign starts again (see 113-115), this time also revolving around a series of attacks on animals in the parish by the probably fictitious Great Wyrley gang (see 111, 120-121). Again, George becomes the prime suspect of the hate campaign as well as the animal mutilations. It is here that the quest for truth about George's guilt or innocence starts.

Right from the start of the prosecution, George's guilt is rather a fictional construct by the Staffordshire police and the Quarter Sessions Court than a proven fact. It seems as if they fabricate their own subjective story and truth about the case, unaware of "the difference between personal opinion and scientific proof, between thinking something and knowing it [...]" (178). In fact, George's guilt is decided right from the outset, and in order to arrive at a plausible explanation of it, they not only combine various pieces of circumstantial and inconsistent evidence, such as a damp coat, footprints, and razor blades, but also manipulate the testimonies[15] intended to prove George's innocence. For instance, the prosecuting barrister, Mr Disturnal asks George to repeat his statements "solely in order to exhibit a theatrical disbelief. His strategy was designed to show that the prisoner was extremely cunning and devious, yet constantly incriminating himself" (185-186).

---

[14] For instance, there are advertisements in the *Cannock Chase Courier*, claiming to be for a dating agency run by George's father (see Julian Barnes 50), and in a Blackpool newspaper, offering the Vicarage for sale by public auction (see 64). Moreover, a feigned confession of having written the anonymous letters, signed by George, appears (see 51).

[15] Other witnesses in favour of him are his father (see Julian Barnes 152, 160, 182, 187-192), mother (see 192-193) and sister (see 193), while the witnesses taking the stand to prove his guilt are representatives of the police like Inspector Campbell (see 151-152) and Constable Cooper (see 156), the orthographical expert Thomas Henry Gurrin (see 159, 176-177), the police surgeon Dr Butter (see 159, 179-180), and the veterinary surgeon Mr Lewis (see 176, 186-187).

In a metafictional comment, George compares the police's and authorities' course of action to writing fiction by arbitrarily combining unconnected story elements, which however results in such a convincing, even 'true' fiction, that George is sentenced to seven years' penal servitude for having maimed a horse:

> [T]he whole story began again: the discovery of the mutilated pony, the search of the Vicarage, the blood-stained clothing, the hairs on the coat, the anonymous letters, the prisoner's arrest and subsequent statements. It was just a story, George knew, something made up from scraps and coincidences and hypotheses; he knew too that he was innocent; but something about the repetition of the story by an authority in wig and gown made it take on extra plausibility. (167)

4.2.2. "Who George Really Is" According to Other People's Stories

> A man's virtues are turned into his faults. Self-control presents itself as secretiveness, intelligence as cunning. And so a respectable lawyer, bat-blind and of slight physique, becomes a degenerate who flits across fields at dead of night, evading the watch of twenty special constables, in order to wade through the blood of mutilated animals. It is so utterly topsy-turvy that it seems logical. (Julian Barnes 327-328)

In the context of the prosecution against George, several newspapers report on it regularly, and Barnes includes them in the form of clippings. For instance, he quotes from the Birmingham *Daily Gazette*'s articles about George's arrest and the horse mutilations (see 153-154), and about his sentence of seven year's penal servitude (see 205). In two other articles about George himself, the same newspaper writes that "[t]he accused man, as his name implies, is of Eastern origin" (153-154), which upsets George because he considers this as a description of a Chinese. Moreover, he is said to have a "swarthy face," looks "essentially Oriental in [his] stolidity," and shows "no sign of emotion" (157).

In order to counterbalance this rather negative and slightly racist representations of George, the reader is also familiarized with his father's opinion, who "knows his son to be a decent and honourable boy" (43), and is pleased with"[t]hese flashes of intelligence coming from a docile boy who is often too much turned in on himself [...]" (57). Additionally, a letter by his uncle conveys a positive view of George too: "I always found him nice and heard of his being clever also. [...] Our friends at that time too felt as we did that Parsees are a very old and cultivated race, and have many good qualities" (213).

To conclude, both the negative and the positive characterizations or 'stories' of George represent each party's subjective truth, and are intended to make the reader aware of the fact that one objective truth about his personality cannot be identified. "His dilemma reminds us that our self-images are constructed not only from the stories that we tell ourselves about who we are but also from the stories that others tell about us" (Holmes 66). Furthermore, they are

in fact fictions, at least from George's point of view. Especially as regards the newspaper reports, he feels that "his life [is] turned into headlines, his story [...] consolidated into [...] fact, his character no longer of his own authorship but delineated by others" (Julian Barnes 204). This statement again implies a metafictional aspect, which becomes especially important in the context of Arthur's investigation of George's case, which is examined in the following chapter.

4.2.3. Sherlock Holmes Investigates the Truth

Although George is released from prison on licence already in 1906 thanks to public outrage and several petitions to the Home Office, his conviction is not overturned and he is denied public pardon. As his reputation and professional life are evidently ruined, he writes a letter to the creator of the famous detective Sherlock Holmes, Sir Arthur Conan Doyle, obviously believing that "anyone with intelligence and guile to devise such complicated fictional crimes must therefore be equipped to solve real ones" (Julian Barnes 291). He asks him to help prove his innocence and clear his name by correcting the errors made by the Staffordshire police, the Quarter Sessions Court and the Home Office. Sir Arthur agrees to take up his case and starts to investigate it by re-examining several pieces of evidence and looking for new ones in order to identify the true culprit.

In the context of Arthur's investigation, metafiction plays a significant role. It seems as if he slipped into Sherlock Holmes' role – with his secretary Alfred Wood as Dr Watson – and thereby into one of his detective stories, which becomes an intertextual element as well; or, viewed from a different angle, he turns one of his novels into a real-life detective story, which actually takes place in a novel. Thus, it is not entirely clear where the boundaries between reality and fictional creation lie. "The frontier between Sir Arthur as investigator and defender of an innocent victim, and Conan Doyle as writer, becomes blurred [...]" (Guignery 130).

This blending of real and fictional investigation is textualized by a series of metafictional comments, which make Arthur's investigation of a real case resemble the composition of one of his novels, and actually constitutes a retelling of George's story into Arthur's personal truth about the case:

> It was like starting a book: you had the story but not all of it, most of the characters but not all of them, some but not all of the causal links. You had your beginning, and you had your ending. There would be a great number of topics to be kept in the head at the same time. Some would be in motion, some static; some racing away, others resisting all the mental energy you could throw at them. Well, he was used to that. (Julian Barnes 332)

On the intertextual level, Arthur's involvement in the case is authenticated by incorporating extracts from several documents[16], which, however also serve the purpose of exposing their function in writing another 'true' story about George.

First, there are Arthur's articles about the case, published in two parts in the *Daily Telegraph* on 11 and 12 January 1907 (see 395-396, 415-417), in which he not only criticizes the police's unjust and racist behaviour, but also describes George as "very shy and nervous [...] [and] a most distinguished student" (416). This makes George "feel like several overlapping people at the same time: a victim seeking redress; a solicitor facing the highest tribunal in the country; and a character in a novel" (416). He is convinced that Arthur has fictionalized some aspects of his personality and that racism never played a significant role in his prosecution. For him this is "all true, and yet untrue; flattering, yet unflattering; believable, yet unbelievable" (416).

Secondly, when reading Arthur's "Statement of the Case against Royden Sharp"[17] (424), whom he suspects to be the real perpetrator, George realizes that his way of detection is strikingly similar to the Staffordshire Constabulary's investigation. Ironically, he actually applied the same technique as the police in order to build a case against Royden Sharp: "And it was all, George decided, the fault of Sherlock Holmes. Sir Arthur had been too influenced by his own creation" (426). The evidence he used is quoted or referred to by means of intertextual elements. Inter alia, it comprises the anonymous hate letters of 1892-1896, 1903 (see 339-340) and 1906 (see 314, 343, 398), Dr Scott's diagnosis of George's astygmatic myopia (see 336-337), the knife most likely used for maiming the horses (see 406), and Sharp's scholastic record, which exposes his mischievous behaviour (see 412). However, all these pieces of evidence are circumstantial and largely hearsay, and "under examination, this turns out to be no less rickety and gimcrack a construct than that which led to Edalji's incarceration" (Jon Barnes 2). In fact, Arthur's efforts to prove George's innocence constitute only an attempt to construct his own truth about the case – just as the police made up their own truth. Thus, two truths collide, and the truth of one party is the lie of the other, even more so because a definite solution to the mystery of the Great Wyrley Outrages is never arrived at.

Thirdly, George is critical of the representation of his case in Arthur's autobiography *Memories and Adventures*, in which he, for example, appears to take the whole credit for

---

[16] Apart from the documents mentioned here, the novel also includes extracts from his letter to Captain Anson reporting on his investigation and expressing his conviction of George's innocence (see Julian Barnes 359), as well as his three-part letter published in the *Daily Telegraph* on 23, 24 and 27 May 1907, in which he expresses his anger at the Report of the Gladstone Committee (see 438).

[17] It was presented to the Home Office in 1907.

George's exoneration for himself, ignoring several other people's efforts and petitions. George considers this account faulty and unreliable because it is obviously too much influenced and shaped by the powers of Arthur's imagination: "George knew from taking witness statements how the constant recounting of events smoothed the edges of stories, [...] made everything more certain than it had seemed at the time" (471-472).

Although Arthur himself is convinced of George's innocence and considers it as the absolute truth, his perfectly rational and logical, but obviously fictional world is a fantasy. Despite George's acquittal of horse mutilation, the Great Wyrley Outrages remain a mystery, just as real life and truth are often mysteries. For some critics, this is proof enough that truth is stranger than fiction. Head, for example argues that "[t]he chief-literary-historical effect of the novel is to discreetly qualify or undermine the Holmesian unequivocal detective fiction, and one of the salutary lessons for Barnes's Conan Doyle is that real life is messier than he imagines" (24). Similarly, Walter states that "Arthur's intervention does not lead to a dramatic, Sherlock Holmes-like closure. There are loose ends, uncertainties and unproven accusations, which allow us to reflect on the difference between the knowability of detective fiction and the unknowability of real life [...]" (par 5).

In conclusion, "Barnes raises questions about the very nature of detection, fabrication and the pursuit of truth [...]" (Bradford 107) by fictionalizing the fictional character of Arthur into his own literary creation. Thereby, he draws attention to the novel's own fictitious nature, lays open the instability of the borderlines between truth and fiction, and "violates its realism to expose the artifice behind it" (Holmes 67).

4.2.4. The Ultimate, Yet Ambiguous Truth

After Arthur's investigation of George's case, the Home Office publishes the Report of the Gladstone Committee, which concedes the errors made in the trial, exposes the evidence used by the police as "*inconsistent, and indeed contradictory*" (Julian Barnes 429), and turns the final official verdict into a free pardon. George is declared innocent of the horse mutilation and later on readmitted to the Rolls by the Incorporated Law Society. At the same time, the committee considers him guilty of having written the anonymous letters of 1903, which is the act of "*an innocent man, but a wrong-headed and malicious man, indulging in a piece of impish mischief*" (430). It also blames him for his own misfortune, and rejects compensation (see 433-434). Thus, George's final verdict not only mentions the dubious nature of the case, but is ambivalent in itself, and therefore reflects the indeterminate status of truth echoing

throughout the novel. George summarizes the content of the report in an "aporia" (Holmes 67), thereby drawing attention to its inherent lack of clarity:

> Innocent yet guilty. Innocent yet wrong-headed and malicious. Innocent yet indulging in impish mischief. Innocent yet deliberately seeking to interfere with the proper investigations of the police. Innocent yet bringing his troubles upon himself. Innocent yet undeserving of compensation. Innocent yet undeserving of an apology. Innocent yet fully deserving of three years' penal servitude. (Julian Barnes 442)

Ironically, it also undermines George's faith in the logic of the law, which, according to him, offers ultimate truth in the form of a perspicuous agreement, decision and explanation because "[t]here is a journey from confusion to clarity" (90).

In order to destabilize even the Home Office's official, yet equivocal version of truth, which is sanctioned by the authorities, Barnes lets a variety of voices rise. For instance, George himself considers the free pardon *"merely a step in the right direction"* (436), but thinks that the accusation of being the writer of the Greatorex letters is *"a slander – an insult ... a baseless insinuation"* (436). He even reflects upon the numerous opinions and unofficial verdicts that have been agreed on so far:

> [T]he *Daily Telegraph* had called the Committee's and the Home Secretary's position *weak, illogical and inconclusive.* The public's attitude [...] was that he *never once had fair play.* The legal profession [...] had supported him. And finally, one of the greatest writers of the age had loudly and continually asserted his innocence. Would these verdicts in time come to outweigh the official one? (442)

Besides, in their letters to the *Daily Telegraph*, Arthur and George's father describe the final verdict as *"absolutely illogical and untenable"* (436) and *"most shocking and heartless"* (436) from a rational and emotional perspective respectively. By contrast, in an interview with the *Staffordshire Sentinel*, Captain Anson expresses his anger at the report's criticism of the police and their allegedly contradictory evidence: "[i]t was [...] *untrue* that the police began from a certainty of Edalji's guilt, and then sought evidence to support that view. [...] Suspicion only *finally became excited against Edalji owing to his commonly-talked-of habits of wandering abroad late at night"* (437). Again, Anson's truth is immediately opposed: in his letter in refutation appearing in the *Daily Telegraph*, George states that the allegations against him have absolutely no basis, and that "he never did *once* 'wander abroad' [...]. There was *no person in the district* less likely to be out at night [...]" (437).

Summing up, all these different reactions again imply polyphony, but, most importantly, none of these people is satisfied with the Home Office's sentence. George's supporters are certain about his innocence, and consider his guilt as a lie, whereas his opponents do so vice-

versa. As each party claims their version to be the truthful one and rejects a consent, an objective and all-embracing truth cannot be got at; but it is probably exactly this conglomerate of subjective convictions that makes up the 'real' nature of truth.

It is only in the paratext that something like the historical truth emerges. In the author's note Barnes not only informs the reader about what happened to the individual characters in real life after the events narrated in the main text, but also says that in 1934, an elderly workman, Enoch Knowles, confessed to be responsible for a hate mail campaign in the vicarage, but did not mention the animal mutilations at all. In an article George wrote for the *Daily Express* in the same year, he again emphasized that "[t]he great mystery, however, remained unsolved" (504) – the truth about the Great Wyrley Outrages has never been uncovered, just as Barnes does not allow his imagination to invent it. Thus, even the paratext echoes the ambivalent nature of truth and the novel's "paradoxical accomplishment of dramatizing history in all of its detail and substantiality while simultaneously sensitizing us to the [...] nebulousness of the past" (Holmes 67).

5. Conclusion

In conclusion, *Arthur & George* not only negotiates actual facts and imagined fictions, but also conjoins them in order to make the reader reflect upon the real status of truth and its relationship to fiction or story-telling, for example, in the context of history, biography, guilt and innocence, spiritualism, love and life itself. In fact, *Arthur & George* is a complex and profound reflection on the often disastrous differences between what we imagine, think, believe, know and can prove, a problem that will probably always exist. Thereby, the readers are made aware of the ambiguous relationship between faithful reconstruction and fictionalized account of historical people and events, between fact and fiction, which are often indistinguishable from each other. Moreover, they most likely realize that it is impossible to reveal one objective truth, which is at best a malleable subjective construct, but actually remains a mystery.

> Barnes gently mocks the Holmesian belief that life is a problem to be solved by logic and close observation. Instead, the story suggests, human justice can never be more than approximate because "truth" – always filtered through one individual consciousness or another – is so fluid a commodity.
> What is real? When is goodness genuine? Can either innocence or love ever be absolute? And what is the nature of Doyle's attachment to spiritualism: a cruel hoax or something more enlightened? Such questions weave throughout the narrative. (Kehe, pars. 13-14)

In order to communicate these messages, Barnes lets the different story levels – the question of guilt and innocence in the unsolved mystery of the Great Wyrley Outrages, or the unsuccessful quest for the truth about love and about spiritualism – reflect this enigmatic nature of reality. Various subjective truths about these issues are conveyed by the different characters' individual voices and convictions. Trying to echo these multiple truths on the discourse level, Barnes uses a variety of discursive devices which combine to form a multifaceted narrative technique.

> Barnes selects, omits, emphasises and interprets. He controls the content and how it reaches the reader. As so often in his novels, he reminds us that history is inexact, partial and fanciful, that it is concerned with fiction as much as fact. The mechanics of detection, the due process of the law, the soothing claims of spiritualism – nothing is quite what it seems. (Taylor, par. 9)

Although "[i]ts realism is less troubled, grounded as it is in the period details and archival documents Barnes uses" (Holmes 48), *Arthur & George* nevertheless seems to be a postmodern novel which works on a metafictional level and "self-consciously and systematically draws attention to its status as an artefact in order to pose questions about the relationship between fiction and reality" (Lethbridge and Mildorf 83). As Barnes suggests, the construction of truth may assume a metafictional dimension, in so far as it can be compared to writing stories, for example, those written about the case and about George by the police, the newspapers and Arthur. This comparison lays open Barnes' conception of the often invisible borderline between truth and fiction.

Viewed from a present-day perspective, this postmodern novel even enters into a dialogue with the reader. As Barnes himself "didn't think of it as a historical novel. […] [but] as a contemporary novel which happened a hundred years ago" (Schiff 71), he was obviously aware of the collision of beliefs and opinions that it would probably entail. The "cultural gap between *Arthur & George*'s turn-of-the-twentieth-century characters and Barnes's twenty-first-century readers" (Holmes 60) results in a discrepancy of knowledge, for example about jurisdiction or spiritualism. This is even pointed out by Arthur because "he also recognized that knowledge never stayed still, and that today's certainties might become tomorrow's superstitions" (Julian Barnes 53). In this way, the impossibility of establishing an eternally valid truth is even communicated on an extratextual and nonfictional level between author and reader.

6. Bibliography

Adams, Tim. "Show Me the Way to Go, Holmes: Julian Barnes' Wonderfully Executed *Arthur & George* Recounts Conan Doyle's Own Detective Adventure." Rev. of *Arthur & George*, by Julian Barnes. *Observer* 26 June 2005. 13 December 2008 <http://www.guardian.co.uk/books/2005/jun/26/fiction>.

Ball, Magdalena. Rev. of Arthur & George, by Julian Barnes. *The Compulsive Reader* 2008. 13 December 2008 <http://www.compulsivereader.com/html/index.php?name=News&file=article&sid=1112>.

Barnes, Jon. "The Pig-chaser's Tale." Rev. of *Arthur & George*, by Julian Barnes. *TLS (Times Literary Supplement)* 8 July 2005. 13 December 2008 <http://tls.timesonline.co.uk/article/0,,25361-1886513.html>.

Barnes, Julian. *Arthur & George*. London: Vintage, 2006.

Bradford, Richard. *The Novel Now: Contemporary British Fiction*. Malden: Blackwell, 2007.

Crumey, Andrew. "Stranger Than Any Fiction." Rev. of *Arthur & George*, by Julian Barnes. *Scotland on Sunday* 3 July 2005. 13 December 2008 <http://living.scotsman.com/books/Stranger-than-any-fiction>.

Guignery, Vanessa. *The Fiction of Julian Barnes*. Houndmills: Palgrave Macmillan, 2006.

Hanks, Robert. "Julian Barnes: Resurrecting Sir Arthur Conan Doyle." Rev. of *Arthur & George*, by Julian Barnes. *Independent* 8 July 2005. 13 December 2008 <http://www.independent.co.uk/arts-entertainment/books/features/julian-barnes-resurrecting-sir-arthur-conan-doyle-497917.html>.

Hawthorn, Jeremy. *Studying the Novel: An Introduction*. 3rd ed. London: Arnold, 1997.

Head, Dominic. "Julian Barnes and a Case of English Identity." *British Fiction Today*. Eds. Philip Tew and Rod Mengham. London: Continuum, 2006. 15-27.

Holmes, Frederick M. *Julian Barnes*. Houndmills: Palgrave Macmillan, 2009.

Jahn, Manfred. *Narratology: A Guide to the Theory of Narrative*. English Department, University of Toronto. 28 May 2005. 20 December 2008 <http://www.uni-koeln.de/~ame02/pppn.htm>.

James, P.D. "Ideal Holmes Exhibition." Rev. of *Arthur & George*, by Julian Barnes. *Times* 9 July 2005. 13 December 2008 <http://entertainment.timesonline.co.uk/tol/arts_and_entertainment/books/article541486.ece>.

Kehe, Marjorie. "How Would Sherlock Holmes Fare in Real Life? This captivating novel by Julian Barnes examines Arthur Conan Doyle's actual foray into criminal justice." Rev. of *Arthur & George*, by Julian Barnes. *Christian Science Monitor* 17 January 2006. 13 December 2008 <http://www.csmonitor.com/2006/0117/p13s01-bogn.html>.

—

Lethbridge, Stefanie, and Jarmila Mildorf. "Prose." *Basics of English Studies: An Introductory Course for Students of Literary Studies in English*. English Departments of the Universities of Tübingen, Stuttgart and Freiburg. 2 March 2004. 20 December 2008 <http://www2.anglistik.uni-freiburg.de/intranet/englishbasics/PDF/Prose.pdf>.

Rafferty, Terrence. "The Game's Afoot." Rev. of *Arthur & George*, by Julian Barnes. *New York Times* 15 January 2006. 13 December 2008 <http://www.nytimes.com/2006/01/15/books/review/15rafferty.html?_r=1&pagewanted=3>.

Schiff, James A. "A Conversation with Julian Barnes." *The Missouri Review* 30.3 (Fall 2007): 60-80. *Project Muse*. 2008. Vienna University Library. 13 December 2008 <http://muse.jhu.edu/>.

Strout, Cushing. "The Case of the Novelist, the Solicitor, and a Miscarriage of Justice." Rev. of *Arthur & George*, by Julian Barnes. *Sewanee Review* 115.1 (Winter 2007): xi-xiii. *Project Muse*. 2008. Vienna University Library. 13 December 2008 <http://muse.jhu.edu/>.

Taylor, Andrew. "A Secret Mystery of History." Rev. of *Arthur & George*, by Julian Barnes. *Independent* 15 July 2005. 13 December 2008 <http://www.independent.co.uk/arts-entertainment/books/reviews/arthur-amp-george-by-julian-barnes-498789.html>.

Walter, Natasha. "Our Mutual Friends." Rev. of *Arthur & George*, by Julian Barnes. *Guardian* 2 July 2005. 13 December 2008 <http://www.guardian.co.uk/books/2005/jul/02/bookerprize2005.bookerprize>.